LOCH EARN

P J G Ransom

A Guide for Visitors,
particularly those going afloat.

Published by the author at:
Woodside
Lochearnhead
Perthshire
FK19 8QD

ISBN 0 9523384 0 8

Loch Earn, looking from Edinample towards Glen Beich.

Introduction

SOME years ago, when Nessie of Loch Ness was all the rage, and the author and his family were a bit younger than they are now, we had a sort of private joke. In the interests of Loch Earn's tourist industry, we decided, someone should spot a monster here. It would, of course, be called 'Ernie'. (And anyone who saw it, the joke went on, would get a premium bond!)

So it was all the greater surprise, one day when driving people home from a childrens' party, to see a full-size monster afloat in the loch.

It turned out to be an artificial monster, something to do with making an advertisment for vodka. You may remember it: anything could happen, and there was the young lady water skiing behind a monster.

Yet that artificial monster was but an extreme example of the great variety of types of vessel attracted to Loch Earn. Although it is less than seven miles long, and under a mile wide, there are to be found upon it, permanently or intermittently: sailing craft including dinghies, keelboats, cruisers and sailboards; power boats, often towing water skiers; smaller outboard boats, inflatables and personal watercraft such as 'jet skis'; anglers' boats and fish farm work barges; rowing boats, kayaks and Canadian canoes; steam launches, sea planes and military assault craft.

To this variety the writer and his family have made their own particular contribution, going afloat over the past fifteen years or so in (or on) steam launches, sailing dinghies, sail boards, outboard runabouts, canoes, a Sportyak dinghy and a playtime rubber dinghy. Not to mention occasional attempts to hold a rod over the water, which generally seem to have resulted only in the fishes' deciding to stay there to be caught by someone else! This is all perhaps some justification for writing about the loch, if only because it nonetheless puts me in a sort of position of neutrality between its principal groups of users, that is to say, water skiers, sailors of racing craft, and anglers. To that I can add experience of boating not only on other lochs in Scotland, but also widely throughout the lakes, rivers, and canals of England, Wales and both parts of Ireland. However use of the water is a compartmented business, and it may still be that while referring to an activity with which I am not personally familiar I have committed some howler or other - if so

Water skiing from Lochearnhead Watersports (Courier, Dundee)

I hope perhaps that I may be forgiven.

Although in the Highlands, Loch Earn is easy of access - about 65 miles from Edinburgh and 55 from Glasgow with their airports, and 28 from Stirling, where there is access to the motorway/dual carriageway network and a main line station.

The great natural beauty of the loch and its surrounding hills combine with accessibility to draw many people to it, to laze on the banks in the sun, picnic on the shore or paddle in the shallows. And to go afloat. Although Loch Earn is small compared with Loch Lomond or Loch Tay, it is large compared with most lakes and reservoirs further south. To have access to such an expanse of water, in such surroundings, is one of the things which makes Loch Earn attractive to water skiers accustomed otherwise only to flooded gravel pits. Yet its conditions of wind and water present a challenge attractive to sailors too. In such things are the seeds of conflict exacerbated by, for instance, the impact of the wash of power boats upon swimmers and anglers. To residents near the loch, visitors represent annoyance in terms of litter on its banks and noise from their boats. They also represent, less obviously, benefit in the greater availability of daily needs - from bread and butter to jobs to pay for them - than could be justified by the permanent population alone. Besides, when you are fortunate enough to live somewhere attractive, it is pleasant to welcome visitors.

If indeed this booklet contributes towards improved understanding between the various users of the loch, and lochside residents too, then it will serve a useful purpose. Its main purpose, though, is to provide visitors with a concise source of information about local conditions. The lack of such sources was a key issue to which attention was drawn in the 1993 report (p. 78) of the Loch Lomond & Trossachs Working Party to the Secretary of State for Scotland about management of the area including Loch Earn

There has been much talk of bye-laws to regulate activities on the loch, without as yet much result. In the meantime there is little that can be done about the irresponsible, but much for those who are inexperienced or ignorant but willing to learn. This book again is a small contribution in that direction. In any event, the loch is not crowded all the time. Although there are certainly plenty of boats around at summer weekends, yet I have taken people out in my boat at 6 pm on a sunny summer evening to have them comment on the peacefulness and tranquillity of the loch.

The Setting

THE origin and meaning of the name 'Earn' are no longer known. They may be associated with settlement here, long ago, of people from Ireland - that is, in Gaelic, Eire. Or they may not. The writer of the description of Comrie parish in the *Old Statistical Account* would go no further than saying '...called *Erne*, in Gaelic *Erinn*, from its westerly situation', and he was writing in the 1790s when Gaelic was still in everyday use in the district.

The origins of the villages at each end of the loch are much clearer, and so are their names, for neither is particularly old. St Fillan himself is said to have preached to the Picts in their fortress at Dundurn, the prominent isolated hill which rises beside the River Earn a mile to the east of St Fillans. That was in the sixth century when he brought Christianity from Ireland. By the end of the eighteenth century the main settlement in the district was high up in Glen Tarken, but the inhabitants were moved down to the end of the loch, a location which from 1817 proved attractive to builders of villas for summer visitors. 'St Fillans was formerly a wretched hamlet, called Portmore; but it is now one of the prettiest spots in Scotland: it is visited by a great number of tourists...' commented Shearer in 1836 in *Antiquities of Strathearn*. Its villas became popular summer residences for wealthy Victorian families who came, after the manner of the period, for months at a time.

Lochearnhead owes its origin to construction of the military road from Stirling to Fort William in the mid-eighteenth century. The *Old Statistical Account* mentioned 'two villages in their infancy' along this road, one of which, 'at the head of Lochearn', was 'extending rapidly'. Its importance was confirmed by construction of the connecting road up from Comrie and St Fillans, and establishment of an inn at the junction.

Prominently in view across the loch from Lochearnhead is Edinample Castle, one of several castles owned early in the seventeenth century by Black Duncan of the Cowl, a notoriously brutal laird whose principal seat was Finlarig Castle, Killin. Edinample Castle has passed through many hands since then, but by contrast Ardvorlich, on the south side of the loch a couple of miles from its head, has been home to the Stewarts of Ardvorlich continuously since the 1580s.

Crannogs

Far more ancient than any of these settlements are the loch's two crannogs, one at each end. Crannogs were once widespread in Scottish lochs: islets which were wholly or partly man-made and date in many cases from the first or second millenium BC. To prehistoric man they evidently meant security, for people and livestock, from human enemies and wild animals such as wolves, and also storage for grain secure from rats and mice. Their use continued until the seventeenth century if not later: the *New Statistical Account* (1838) notes that the crannog at the east end of Loch Earn was 'latterly occupied by the family of Ardvorlich, who had an occasional residence and a granary there'.

On shore close by the crannog at the west end of the loch are the ruins of St Blane's chapel. St Blane was a sixth century saint whose name is associated with Dunblane. Low walls of an ancient rectangular building remain, aligned on the crannog and suggesting that the locations of the two are related.

Ian Morrison, in *Landscape with Lake Dwellings: The Crannogs of Scotland*, associates the siting of crannogs with adjacent agricultural land. Shelter from storms was also important, and in this connection it is intriguing to note that while the crannog at the west end of Loch Earn is in the spot most sheltered from the prevailing south-west wind, that at the east end, called Neish Island, could scarcely be more exposed. It is close to the north shore: perhaps its original inhabitants had their farms where St Fillans now stands.

By late mediaeval times this crannog carried the fortified stronghold of the Neish clan from which it takes its name, and although King James IV gave orders in 1490 for its destruction, it was evidently rebuilt at least in part. The Neishes engaged in intermittent tribal warfare with the Macnabs to the north, the climax coming in 1612 when they waylayed and robbed the Macnab chief's servants en route from Crieff to Killin with Christmas cheer. To the Macnabs this was the last straw: they carried a boat over the hills, rowed out to Neish Island by night, massacred the Neishes, decapitated their chief and several others and carried the heads back as an offering to the chief of their own clan.

The story has been told and re-told in print,

recently by Archie McKerracher who in *Perthshire in History and Legend* adds the results of recent research. It describes one of several such bloodthirsty events associated with the district, which four or five centuries ago was no less turbulent than many other parts of the Highlands.

Those who wish to find out more about the history of this part of the world, in times of harmony as well as strife, will find much of interest in the Breadalbane Folklore Centre, due to open at Killin in June 1994, and in the Rob Roy & Trossachs Visitor Centre at Callander.

Hydro-electricity

The water power resources of the Highlands have been used to generate electricity since the 1890s, and a general programme to develop them followed passage of the Hydro-Electric Development (Scotland) Act, 1943. This established the North of Scotland Hydro-Electric Board (which was eventually privatised as Scottish Hydro-Electric plc in 1990). The board proceeded by means of a series of 'Constructional Schemes' authorised by the Secretary of State; Scheme no. 25, Breadalbane Project, was authorised in 1953, and the St Fillans section of this scheme incorporates Loch Earn.

Water which would otherwise flow naturally to Loch Tay is diverted to Lednock Power Station and Loch Lednock reservoir, which is also fed by water from the Rivers Almond and Lednock. Thence it then passes to St Fillans, being joined en route by further supplies from Glens Boltachan, Tarken and Beich. Like so much of this and other hydro-electric schemes, extensive but un-ostentatious, St Fillans power station is hidden from view beneath the ground, the central point in the rabbit warren of tunnels and aqueducts which feed it. Its outfall is into Loch Earn. The whole of the loch serves as a reservoir for Dalchonzie power station: the weir at St Fillans, across the River Earn just below its natural exit from the loch, diverts much of its flow into a 3-mile tunnel to the power station. This tunnel is 11ft 6 in. diameter, comparable to a London tube train tunnel.

Dalchonzie and St Fillans power stations were commissioned in 1958 and 1957 respectively. Dalchonzie has a capacity of 4 Megawatts; the capacity of St Fillans, with a higher head, is 21 Megawatts - equivalent, that is, to 21,000 single-bar electric fires, or the electricity requirements of a

Neish Island crannog, St Fillans, with Four Seasons Hotel jetty in left foreground.

smallish country town.

All of these hydro-electric installations are controlled remotely from Southern Hydro Group's control room at Clunie Power Station, Pitlochry. This has 27 main storage reservoirs and 25 power stations under its command: its operators endeavour to balance precipitation, actual and forecast, against demand for electricity.

Fish Farming

When you buy Rainbow Trout in Marks & Spencer or Sainsbury's, it may well have come from Drummond Estates' fish farm in Ardveich Bay, Loch Earn. This is one of the largest trout farms in Scotland, producing 370 tons of trout a year. The fish arrive at Ardveich as fingerlings and grow to full size over 8 to 12 months, depending on water temperature, and so upon the time of year.

Fish have to be fed every day, and someone from the farm's staff (five full-time, two part-time, two on security) is present round the clock, even on Christmas Day. To service the farm they use two twin-hulled barges. One of these is used exclusively to take food out to the cages, the other to move the cages around.

The farm was established about 1980 by United Biscuits in pursuit of diversification. It was more successful in producing fish than in selling them: Drummond Estates, the riparian landowner, bought the farm in 1984, and sales have subsequently improved, for dietary customs are changing and more and more people are turning from meat to fish.

Ardveich Bay fish farm sells all its fish wholesale and is not open to the public. However Drummond Estates' other fish farm, near Comrie, which also produces Rainbow Trout, does do retail sales and is open to the public all round the year.

Canoeists at St Fillans, looking towards Achray House Hotel.

The Approaches

LOCH Earn is approached from the south by the A84 from Stirling and Callander, from the east by the A85 from Perth, Crieff and Comrie, and from the north by the A85 from Killin and Crianlarich.

Prior to the reorganisation of local government in the 1970s it lay entirely within Perthshire: subsequently it has been divided between Tayside and Central Regions. The course of the boundary is shown on the accompanying map; it is also the boundary between Perth & Kinross and Stirling Districts, St. Fillans and Balquhidder Community Councils, and Tayside and Central Scotland Police Forces. Perthshire Tourist Board promotes tourism around the eastern part of the loch, Loch Lomond Stirling & Trossachs Tourist Board around the western. The whole area around the loch remains 'Perthshire' in postal addresses.

For some years the regional boundary in the vicinity of Lochearnhead followed the loch shore, a situation which produced numerous anomalies. For example, in the event of an incident on the water requiring the attention of the police, it was a matter for the Tayside Police, whose nearest station is 14 miles away at Comrie, although the Lochearnhead police station is only a few hundred yards from the loch. The loch was in the area of one planning authority, the land in another. When the water level was high, the border was some way out into the loch, but when it was low a rim of Tayside shingle was exposed. And so on.

The boundary was altered to its present course in April 1990, to follow the middle of the loch rather than edge. The alteration eliminated the many anomalies of its previous course, and it is to be hoped that reorganisation of local government will not result in a new border along the shore.

Access

The foreshore of Loch Earn is all owned by somebody, and so are all jetties and slipways. Access across the foreshore for launching boats is dependent on the goodwill of riparian landowners. Fortunately many of the lochside establishments have slipways and jetties for use by customers and/or the general public - details are given below.

Other jetties are private. Launching off the beach,

Sailing from Lochearnhead Watersports jetty.
(Loch Lomond, Stirling & Trossachs Tourist Board)

where a road happens to run nearby, is generally discouraged - particularly for motor craft. Indeed launching of speed or motor boats off the beach is specifically forbidden along the south shore road where it passes through Ardvorlich estate.

The riparian owners own not only the beach but also the adjoining bed of the loch. This is a fairly academic point so far as the deep water is concerned, but important in the shallows where moorings are laid and jetties built. The lengthy history of use of the loch by boats - some details of it are given below - suggests a prescriptive right of navigation, that is, one based on long use.

Training in Power and Sail

Those without experience of boating should certainly seek formal training before launching. The proposition that 'if you can drive a car, you can drive a boat' is fallacious, indeed dangerous. For a start, boats steer by swinging the back about, not the front, and have neither brake pedal nor handbrake.

The source of information about training in handling boats is the Royal Yachting Association. This has a vast range of instructional literature and videos, and provides details of the hundreds of RYA-recog-

13

nised training establishments. These are divided broadly into those which deal with motor cruising & power boats, dinghy & keelboat sailing, windsurfing, and coastal cruising. On Loch Earn specifically, RYA-recognised training takes the form of the Loch Earn Sailing Club's annual youth training week every summer. RYA Instructors' Courses are also held at the sailing club. Half-day introductory sailing courses in Wayfarers with an RYA-qualified instructor are available at Lochearnhead Watersports Centre.

Courses offered within RYA training schemes commence at the introductory level and become progressively more advanced. Participants with experience join at whatever level they themselves consider to be appropriate. Linked with the RYA power boat training schemes are the British Water Ski Federation Ski Boat Driver courses: these are offered by Lochearnhead Watersports Centre.

Lochearnhead Hotel (left) & jetty; The Boathouse restaurant to the right.

Clachan Cottage Hotel, slip and jetty, used by BCA Activities.

Waterside Facilities

BELOW are facilities around Loch Earn, starting at Lochearnhead, and based on information kindly supplied by the establishments concerned.

Lochearnhead Watersports, Lochearnhead, Perthshire; 0567 830330. Watersports centre with water skiing (wetsuit provided): beginners' lessons, ski tows, boats by the hour with driver & instruction, slalom course, BWSF-approved ski school; Canadian canoes, kayaks and sailing dinghies for hire, with instruction when needed. Popular for group bookings where participants have a chance to try, under skilled supervision, any of the above activities in combination and also marine jet bikes, archery and quad biking with a barbecue in the evening - groups include staff outings, staff incentives, client entertainment and the Regular Army, Territorials and Cadets. Licensed café and lochside lawn; jetty and slipway (no launching of power boats: skiing is behind the centre's own boats); beach where sailboards may be launched. Ski-boat driver instruction. Water skiing and other water sports for the disabled.

Loch Earn Lodges, Lochearnhead, Perthshire; 0567 830211. Self-catering chalets with (for customers) free use of slipway and jetty, and three moorings for boats up to about 16 ft long.

Lochearnhead Hotel, Lochearnhead, Perthshire. 0567 830229. Hotel with restaurant, bistro bar and self-catering 'Lochside Cottages'. Moorings for guests. Slipway and jetty for power boats, as many as can get alongside jetty - guests have priority, available to others with power boats on payment. Also available by arrangement for sailing boats, anglers' boats and sailboards.

The Boathouse, Lochearnhead, Perthshire; 0567 830306. Lochside licensed restaurant for snacks and meals; jetty; slipway available by prior arrangement.

Clachan Cottage Hotel, Lochearnhead, Perthshire, FK19 8PU; 0567 830247. Hotel with restaurant, lounge bar and pub. Slipway, jetty and moorings free to guests; slipway and jetty available to others on payment, in return for voucher redeemable in restaurant or bars. Space limited but can be booked.

Jetty also used by:

BCA Activities, Lochside, Lochearnhead, Perthshire, FK19 8PU; 0567 830367. Water skiing: tows, lessons, slalom, wet suit hire, for individuals and groups. Regular customers join club to get discounts on charges, access to slalom course (by arrangement) and seasonal moorings. Canoe hire. Base at Clachan Cottage Hotel, using hotel jetty. Limited range of accessories for sale (eg., ski ropes, gloves, wet socks, spark plugs and oil); skis etc. obtained to order. On land for groups of eight or more, off-road go-kart racing and quad bike driving. Probably to be re-named **PA Leisure**.

MacKinnon's Garden Shop, St Blanes, Lochearnhead, Perthshire 0567 830205, adjacent to shop is Caravan Club certificated location for up to five touring caravans (members only), overlooking loch with access to shore. No launching.

Earnknowe, Lochearnhead, Perthshire, FK19 8PY; 0567 830238. Self-catering holiday cottages with fine views over loch and use of jetty (shared with Hertfordshire Scouts, below) free to guests. Dinghy (12 ft) with outboard available for daily hire to guests.

Lochearnhead Scout Station, bookings to Mrs MacDiarmaid, 16 Roseacre Gardens, Sylvan Way, Welwyn Garden City, Herts; 0707 324967. Former railway station adapted as centre for outdoor activities by Hertfordshire Scouts, who use loch for sailing (sharing use of jetty at Earnknowe), canoeing and board sailing; centre available also to other groups.

Loch Earn Sailing Club, hon. secretary Angus McIlquham, 15 Birks Court, Law, Carluke, ML8 5HZ; 0698 375018. Sailing club, new members welcome, premises on north shore about $1^{1}/_{2}$ miles w. of St Fillans. Facilities for members: slipways, jetties, moorings, clubhouse with panoramic view of loch and tea-making facilities, changing rooms, lockers etc., and caravan site for members' caravans. Racing throughout the summer. No motor boats or water skiing.

Four Seasons Hotel, St Fillans, Perthshire, PH6 2NF; 0764 685333. Hotel with restaurant, bar and chalets; slipway and jetty for hotel guests; no jet skis.

Achray House Hotel, St Fillans, Perthshire, PH6 2NF; 0764 685231. Hotel with restaurant and bar; foreshore (across which small boats might be launched) and jetty for use by guests.

Moorings at Loch Earn Sailing Club.

Looking west from entrance to River Earn, with Drummond Arms jetty.

Drummond Arms Hotel, St Fillans, Perthshire, PH6 2NF; 0764 685212. Hotel with restaurant and bars. Slipway and jetties available free to guests, and to others on payment (no jet skis). Passenger trip boat for guests. Moorings may be added, and so may rowing boats for hire.

Loch Earn Moorings. C. Campbell-Crawford, Homeport, Laggan Road, Crieff, Perthshire, PH7 4JL; 0764 652712. Up to fifteen moorings at St Fillans (by arrangement with riparian landowner the Crieff Hydro Hotel), for seasonal hire or shorter periods if available; sailing boats, inboard motor boats and steam launches preferred. Slipway and jetty for customers, also changing rooms, toilets, and shore for camping and barbecues; static caravan for hire with free use of slipway and jetty. Moorings supplied and laid.

Loch Earn Caravan Park, South Shore Road, St Fillans, Perthshire; 0764 685270. Caravan park with mini-market and Korki's Bar; 260 static caravans and 30 pitches for touring caravans and motor caravans; deep-water slipway and floating jetty with moorings alongside, for use by customers. Largest and noisiest power boats unwelcome: they are in any event unsuited to the loch.

Board sailors take advantage of the breeze.
(Loch Lomond, Stirling & Trossachs Tourist Board)

Fuel: No fuel is available at the lochside: the nearest supplies are filling stations in Lochearnhead and Comrie.

Accomodation: Full details of accomodation available in the district, including many other establishments in addition to those mentioned above, are to be found in the accomodation guides published annually by Loch Lomond, Stirling & Trossachs Tourist Board (covering Lochearnhead) and Perthshire Tourist Board (covering St Fillans).

Other facilities in Lochearnhead include Post Office/shop, Village Shop, Earn Rest (bar/café/filling station/gift shop/caravan park), Glenogle Tweeds shop, Highland Taste Scottish Foods at Glenogle Farm, St Angus's Episcopal Church, with Church of Scotland services also; and in St Fillans, Post Office/village shop, St Fillans Golf Club, St Fillans Caravan Park, Dundurn Parish Church.

Public Transport: buses, to St Fillans from Crieff and Lochearnhead from Callander.

Water Skiing at Lochearnhead. (Loch Lomond, Stirling & Trossachs Tourist Board)

On the Water

THERE is no navigation authority for Loch Earn, although there is a possibility that bye-laws may be introduced to regulate its use by boats: to this subject I return later.

In the meantime, in the absence of formal regulation, responsible behaviour by everyone on the loch is vital for the safety of all.

Boats should carry adequate third party insurance. Adequate means cover for £1/2 million or more. Many owners of slipways enquire about this before giving their permission to launch boats.

Non-swimmers and children should wear buoyancy aids. So indeed should everyone, for most activities afloat on this loch. Put them on while still ashore, for it is when getting into a boat, or out of it, that people are most likely to fall in. The water is exceptionally cold, cold enough to incapacitate quickly even a strong swimmer

Those in charge of boats should be sober. Boats should go slowly through moorings, and when in the

LOCH EARN

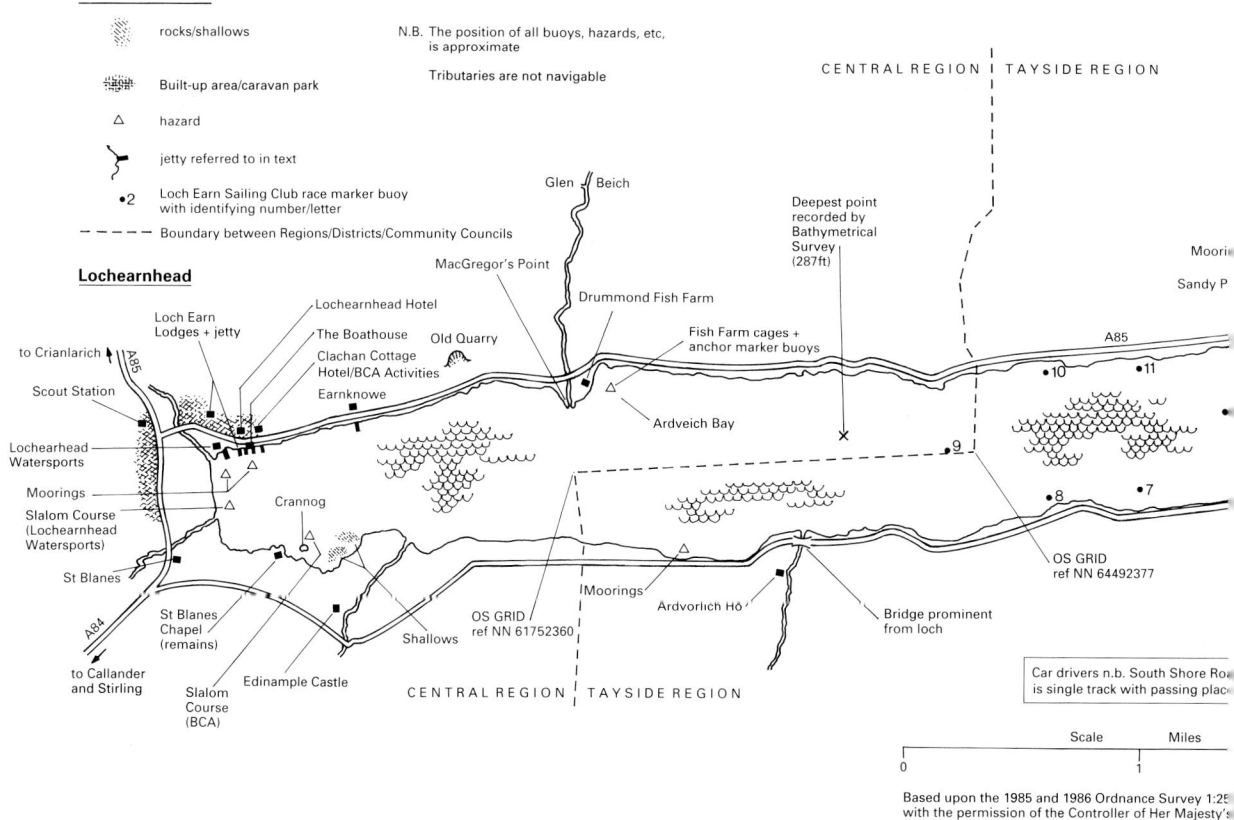

- rocks/shallows
- Built-up area/caravan park
- hazard
- jetty referred to in text
- •2 Loch Earn Sailing Club race marker buoy with identifying number/letter
- – – – Boundary between Regions/Districts/Community Councils

N.B. The position of all buoys, hazards, etc, is approximate

Tributaries are not navigable

CENTRAL REGION | TAYSIDE REGION

Lochearnhead

Glen Beich
MacGregor's Point
Drummond Fish Farm
Deepest point recorded by Bathymetrical Survey (287ft)
Loch Earn Lodges + jetty
Lochearnhead Hotel
The Boathouse
Clachan Cottage Hotel/BCA Activities
Old Quarry
Fish Farm cages + anchor marker buoys
Earnknowe
to Crianlarich
A85
Scout Station
Lochearhead Watersports
Moorings
Slalom Course (Lochearnhead Watersports)
St Blanes
Crannog
St Blanes Chapel (remains)
A84
to Callander and Stirling
Edinample Castle
Slalom Course (BCA)
Shallows
OS GRID ref NN 61752360
Moorings
Ardvorlich Hô
CENTRAL REGION | TAYSIDE REGION
Ardveich Bay
•10 •11
•9
•8 •7
OS GRID ref NN 64492377
Bridge prominent from loch

Car drivers n.b. South Shore Road is single track with passing places

Scale Miles
0   1

Based upon the 1985 and 1986 Ordnance Survey 1:25 with the permission of the Controller of Her Majesty's Office. © Crown Copyright

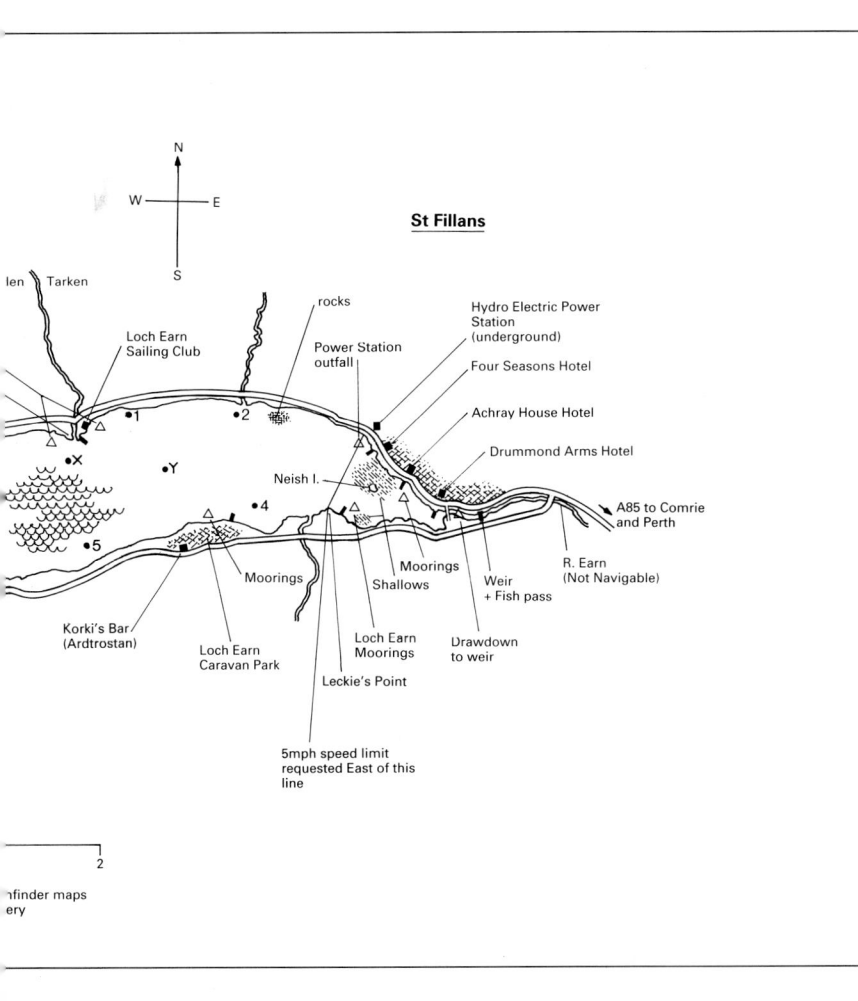

[Map of Loch Earn / St Fillans area with labels: N/W/E/S compass; Glen Tarken; Loch Earn Sailing Club; rocks; Power Station outfall; Hydro Electric Power Station (underground); Four Seasons Hotel; Achray House Hotel; Drummond Arms Hotel; Neish I.; A85 to Comrie and Perth; R. Earn (Not Navigable); Moorings; Weir + Fish pass; Shallows; Moorings; Korki's Bar (Ardtrostan); Loch Earn Caravan Park; Loch Earn Moorings; Leckie's Point; Drawdown to weir; 5mph speed limit requested East of this line; points marked 1, 2, X, Y, 4, 5]

vicinity of swimmers and anglers.

The usual 'rules of the road' are applied by custom on this loch as on other inland waters (even though the Collision Regulations apply formally only at sea, or on waterways with a navigable connection to the sea, which Loch Earn lacks). So motor vessels give way to sail, to other motor vessels approaching from starboard, and so on.

The British Water Ski Federation incorporates an abridgement of the Collision Regulations in its own comprehensive safety recommendations. All ski-boat drivers should certainly comply with these, not least with that requirement for a second person in the boat to watch the skier while the driver concentrates on the water ahead. These and much more (such as essential equipment to be carried on board) are covered by the BWSF's Ski Boat Driver Award courses.

Similarly, sailors who have learned

Loch Earn Sailing Club, from the south shore.

at any RYA-recognised training establishment have been taught the usual 'rules of the road' and expect to follow them; racing takes place under international yacht racing rules.

Hazards, and lack of them

One of the attractions of Loch Earn is its general freedom from hazards in the water: such as there are are indicated on the map and described below.

Lochearnhead on a summer day. (Loch Lomond, Stirling & Trossachs Tourist Board)

In the absence of a navigation authority, they are unmarked. Much of the loch is deep, its bed shelving steeply downwards close off shore, though both ends are shallow. The angles at which fences descend into the loch give a guide to its depth.

The least obvious, and so perhaps most serious, hazard is the weather - not for severity, but for changeability. Although there are many days when the weather is settled, there are also many when showers succeed sunshine and squalls intermingle with calms. Each day is usually different from the next: one should never (in the author's experience) neglect to cover the boat over properly, however fine the evening, on the grounds of coming down again tomorrow, because a local variant of Murphy's Law will inevitably produce force nine by morning and it will be too rough even to get out to the boat in the dinghy. (A further variant of the same Law says that whenever you decide to haul out, when it comes to the point it will be raining!)

The prevailing wind is from the South West, which seems transformed into a west wind by the time it is half way down the loch. This and the less common east wind tend to blow steadily: when, unusually, the wind comes from North or South over

Sailing in summer.

the hills it is often much more fluky. There is a chill factor in the wind to be taken into account too: warm clothes are needed on the loch, particularly on sunny but windy days when, in places sheltered from the wind, it is warm.

The water level varies according to season, rainfall and the needs of hydro-electric power generation. It is monitored continuously by Scottish Hydro-Electric plc at its Clunie control room, and indicated on a gauge beside St Fillans Power Station outfall. The crest of the fixed weir at St Fillans is 317.5 ft above Ordnance Datum; the company aims for a water level in summer of 316 ft, and in winter of 315.5 ft, to allow for rainfall and snow. Efficient operation, fortunately, is compatible with responsibility to the community. As I write this, the level has been allowed to fall considerably to assist a lochside enterprise where repairs are needed below the normal water level.

The highest level recorded since the hydro-electric scheme was commissioned is 322.6 ft, the lowest 314.4 ft - both of them in the month of February, in 1990 and 1979 respectively. The company has a statutory right to draw the level down to as low as 312.5 ft in the event, for instance, of repairs being needed to the tunnel entrance at St Fillans.

The loch being fresh water, it becomes more choppy than salt water for the same strength of wind. There are no harbours of refuge, nor do any slow-flowing rivers enter the loch to provide refuge or sheltered moorings. Neish Island does provide shelter from a strong westerly, and there is a wind shadow at either end of the loch according to wind direction.

The best local weather forecast that the author has found is that available over the telephone on 0891 500423.

Fog on the water is virtually unknown. There are no overhead power lines to limit air draft, and only one bridge, over the entrance to the river at St Fillans, which small craft pass beneath without difficulty.

There is no general rescue service. Lochearnhead Watersports has a rescue boat on standby whenever activities are taking place there. Races organised by Loch Earn Sailing Club have a rescue boat in attendance, and so do sailing activities by Hertfordshire Scouts. Fish farm employees have been to the assistance of many boats in difficulties, but are under no obligation to do so.

Now to consider specific hazards along the loch, with reference to the map on the centre pages.

At St Fillans, the River Earn as it leaves the loch is generally deep enough for boats as far as the weir. Sometimes, however, there is a powerful drawdown towards the weir, which is hidden from view round the first bend, unprotected and without warning notices. Canoeists, particularly, should be wary.

St Fillans Community Council requests a maximum speed of 5 mph for boats east of Leckie's Point - to minimise noise and wash - and also that power boats and jet skis everywhere should operate at least 100 yards off-shore.

There are shallows all round the shore at St Fillans, and particularly between Neish Island and the north shore where the island's original inhabitants perhaps had a causeway. Those without local knowledge should keep south of the island. About 200 yd west of the island an unmarked rock is close enough to the surface to be danger to keelboats.

The outfall from St Fillans power station produces a strong current into the loch when the station is generating. For it to reach full power from start-up takes about five minutes.

Buoys which bear the painted letters LESC and a number, at intervals up the loch, are the sailing club's racing marks, around which race officers set courses according to the wind.

At the fish farm, buoys around the farm are marker buoys for the anchors which hold the cages in position. Propeller-driven craft should keep outside these to avoid tangling with the mooring lines - about six of them to each block of cages.

The east side of the bay off Edinample is shallow. At its west side, I have often passed safely between crannog and shore in boats drawing 2 ft or so, while keeping a wary eye on the rocky bed of the loch seen through the clear water.

Buoys at the western end of the loch mark the two water-ski slalom courses, both private - one in the bay off Edinample, the other off Lochearnhead Watersports Centre.

Sailing at St Fillans. (Perthshire Tourist Board/Graham Hood)

The Loch Itself

LIKE many other large lochs, Loch Earn occupies a long, narrow, steep-sided basin eroded long ago by a glacier. The principal burns that enter from the sides flow into it over cones of detritus which project into the loch: the sailing club takes advantage of one of these to locate its clubhouse and find shelter for moorings, and the fish farm shelters from the prevailing wind in the lee of another.

To Loch Earn there came in 1900 Sir John Murray FRS and Mr F. P. Pullar, who had commenced as a spare-time self-imposed task a systematic survey of the Scottish fresh-water lochs. Murray had spent many years surveying ocean basins; his attention had been drawn to fresh water lochs by marked differences he had found between the sea lochs of the West Coast and the fresh water lochs of the Caledonian Canal (Ness, Oich and Lochy). His proposal in 1883 for a full-scale survey was turned down by the government - the Admiralty did such work only in the interest of navigation, the Ordnance Survey worked only on land. Murray and Pullar started their own survey in 1897.

Loch Earn had already been partially sounded in the mid-1880s by J. S. Grant Wilson, researching into correlation between glaciation and Perthshire lochs, and by Mr Sandison of St Fillans. Sir John Murray and F.P. Pullar personally took 150 soundings in 1900.

Early in 1901 tragedy intervened: Pullar was involved in an accident on ice, and drowned. Murray was only persuaded to continue when Pullar's father undertook to finance the 'Bathymetrical Survey of the Scottish Fresh-Water Lochs' by way of a memorial. The results of the survey were published at intervals, and a comprehensive account with maps appeared in 1910.

The staff of the main survey took 500 more soundings in Loch Earn in May 1902. With its surface 317.2 ft above sea level, the greatest depth that they recorded was 287 ft (Grant Wilson had recorded 288 ft) south of Dalkenneth and almost one third of a mile off-shore - nearly half way across. The soundings confirmed that the bed of the loch was a simple basin. A detailed map was produced: the curious may find a framed copy hanging in the Lochearnhead Hotel. From the point of view of present-day boaters, one might wish that the surveyors had spent more time finding out how shallow the loch is at the edges, rather than how deep in the middle! But the survey was a remarkable achievement.

The maximum depth of Loch Earn placed it 16th in order of depth of the 562 lochs surveyed in the complete programme: the deepest was shown to be Loch Morar at 1,017 ft. Loch Earn's length of 6.46 miles made it 18th longest (the longest being Loch Awe at 25.47 m.); its area of 3.91 sq. miles made it 15th largest, the largest of all being Loch Lomond, 27.45 sq. miles.

As well as depths of lochs, the Bathymetrical Survey concerned itself with other features such as water temperature, chemical composition of the water, and biology. And also with seiches.

A seiche (in case you did not know, like the author until recently) is a stationary oscillation of the water in a lake about a nodal line or lines part-way along, which results in a rise and fall of the water level at the ends - apparent tides. Likely causes include changes in barometric pressure, wind, rain and minor earthquakes. Much important research into the nature of seiches, recorded in the Bathymetrical Survey, was done in the 1900s by Professor Chrystal of Ardtrostan, who had instruments to record fluctuations in water level at Ardtrostan, St Fillans, Lochearnhead and elsewhere: and in connection with seiches Loch Earn has its moment of glory, a mention in the *Encyclopaedia Britannica* (1963 edition) along with the Lake of Geneva where the phenomenon was first observed.

Water Quality

The quality of water throughout the entire Earn catchment is the concern of the Tay River Purification Board. This is responsible for protecting and improving the water environment. It regulates discharges into the loch and its tributaries. Its programme of bacteriological monitoring of waters used for bathing and recreation includes the loch, where results for 1993 were good, complying with European Community bathing water standards.

The board is particularly interested in concentrations of plant nutrients, especially phosphorus. Levels of phosphorus in Loch Earn are at or slightly above what is acceptable, and developments likely to aggravate this are tightly controlled - consent was withheld for discharge from a proposed new fish farm.

Flows and Floods

The purification board also monitors river flows at gauging stations, co-operating with Scottish Hydro-Electric plc. Hydro-Electric itself has a statutory obligation not to draw water at its intakes unless certain minimum 'compensation flows' are present in the natural watercourses downstream. These flows vary according to season, and the needs of migrating fish. Sluices beside St Fillans weir allow the compensation flow through to the River Earn when the level of the loch is so low that no water, or insufficient, is coming over the weir.

Average annual rainfall has tended to increase over recent decades, and information gained at the purification board's gauging stations is used to warn residents downstream when floods are imminent, such as those of January 1993.

These resulted from a sudden thaw after heavy snowfall. Loch Earn itself floods in such conditions. Hydro-Electric does not deliberately retain water in it at such times: good community relations and commercial interest coincide, for to a generator of hydro-electricity, water lost over the weir is a resource gone to waste. Further, during the worst of the January 1993 floods, St Fillans power station did not generate for four to five days, so that Loch Earn was being fed solely by its own natural catchment.

Regional councils have powers to take steps to prevent or mitigate flooding.

Loch Earn is said never to freeze over. Certainly in the author's observation a spell cold enough to cause Loch Lubnaig to freeze over leaves Loch Earn virtually untouched. The eastern end of the loch, from St Fillans as far as Ardtrostan, is recorded as having frozen sufficiently during the winter of 1894-5 for a curling match to be played upon it. That was the winter when Windermere was frozen for weeks from end to end. (Oddly, the night after the above was written in February 1994 was cold enough for ice to form at both ends of Loch Earn - the first for years.)

The loch in winter.

Fishing

FISHING on Loch Earn is by permit only. The River Earn Catchment Area Protection Order, made in 1990 by the Secretary of State for Scotland, prohibits fishing on Loch Earn without legal rights.

To enable visitors to the area to enjoy the ancient art of angling on Loch Earn, the principal riparian landowners have leased the fishing rights and the management of the fishing on Loch Earn to the St Fillans & Loch Earn Angling Association.

This association currently has a brown trout stocking programme, to improve the fishing on the loch, and this programme is funded primarily through the sale of permits to anglers. Day or weekly permits are on sale at the Post Offices at St Fillans and Lochearnhead and the local hotels and shops in the two villages.

The fishing season is from 15 March to 6 October inclusive.

Anglers are reminded that wardens, representing the Angling Association and the riparian landowners, are authorised to examine permits at all times, and to ensure that all anglers fishing have the relevant permit.

The above information has kindly been provided by the angling association.

Water Skiing off Lochearnhead. (STB/The Still Moving Picture Co.)

Boating Past and Present

THE earliest inhabitants of central Perthshire are said to have arrived by water in western Scotland in the 4th and 3rd millenia BC, and then to have made use of lochs in their lines of communication as they travelled eastwards (M.E.C.Stewart, *The Prehistory of Perthshire*, Transactions of the Perthshire Society of Natural Science 1973). At a period when the land was covered by dense forest containing wolves and bears, travel by boat along a loch was doubtless the preferable option. One imagines the inhabitants of those days moving around through the forest as much as possible by water, in a manner similar to Red Indians in Canada before Europeans arrived. Crannog dwellers certainly used dugout canoes and skin covered coracles, and later on they had clinker-built boats.

A curious feature of accounts of the Neish Island massacre is that there is often said to have been then but one boat on Loch Earn, and that kept by the Neishes on their island. This seems to me a landsman's explanation of the Macnab's need to carry a boat over the hills. Probably the Neishes had plenty of boats, but no doubt they did make sure that not one was left lying around on the mainland beach overnight.

During the end of the eighteenth century and the early part of the nineteenth, large boats carried limestone down the loch. The limestone was quarried from the hillside above the north shore near Lochearnhead, and calcined at St Fillans in kilns - presumably those of which the remains can be seen beside the Four Seasons Hotel. The end-product, lime for fertiliser, was much in demand by the farms further down Strathearn.

It was largely to make distribution of the lime easier that there came at this period a succession of proposals for a canal from Loch Earn to the Tay. The most ambitious, surveyed in 1806-7, would have run via Comrie and Crieff. Below Crieff, however, it was not to take the obvious route down Strathearn to the Firth of Tay, but to run across country via Methven to the Tay at Perth, with a branch from Methven to Stanley and Dunkeld. It was never built.

From 1819 onwards the St Fillans Highland Society organised Highland games, among the earliest to be held anywhere. It was for ease of access to the games field that a footbridge was first built across the River Earn where it leaves the loch. Besides many events of the type which remain familiar, these early games included a two-mile boat race on the loch.

Young Edwin Landseer, on his way to attend the games in 1824, was rowed down the loch from Lochearnhead by a party of Highlanders, men women and children. They entertained him with stories of the fairies which inhabited its shores, to the accompaniment of the distant sound of the pipes.

By the latter part of the century the loch had become very popular with anglers. 'The loch swarms with boats at this end. There ought not to be a trout left, so much are the waters lashed' wrote Tina Roberts, who had taken Lake Cottage at St Fillans for the summer of 1880, to her son in New Zealand. She and her party went to Ardvorlich by boat, rowed by a boatman.

Loch Earn was unusual in having no steamer service in Victorian times, when almost every loch of any size seemed to have one, even some, such as Loch Maree, which were much more remote. It was not until 1922 that a passenger motor vessel, *Queen of Loch Earn*, was placed on the loch to run pleasure cruises in connection with charabanc tours. She had two Rolls Royce petrol engines and went up and down the loch twice a day to a schedule which allowed a youthful Ewen Cameron, of Lochearnhead, to travel down to St Fillans and enjoy a round of golf. Her piers were, at Lochearnhead, where the watersports centre now is, and at St Fillans, immediately south of the entrance to the river. She was eventually withdrawn after the 1936 season.

Latterly, during 1989-90, a trip boat for 10 or 11 people operated at Lochearnhead, and at the Drummond Arms, St Fillans, an electric launch preceded the present cabin cruiser.

Sailing

'An Unexploited Sailing Elysium' was how *Country Life* for 15 August 1968 headlined an article about the inland lochs of Scotland, with the emphasis on Loch Earn. Nonetheless the Loch Earn Sailing Club had originated two decades earlier, formed by Crieff and Perth people, with an assorted fleet. It operated at first from the south shore at St Fillans, close to where Loch Earn Moorings now are, and moved to its present premises at Sandy Point about 1952.

Sailors find Loch Earn a good loch for racing, par-

Flying Fifteens race to the head of the loch, probably during the late 1960s. (STB/ The Still Moving Picture Co.)

ticularly for its wave formation: although waves may run up to 4 ft high, there are seldom rollers. The varying winds test sailors' skills. So the club was successful in promoting racing - World Hornet championships were held on Loch Earn in 1966, and Flying Fifteen Northern championships the following year.

Flying Fifteens are still popular here; there are now about twenty six sailing from the club. There are also some twenty 'cruiser-type' boats, including six Yeomans, and about twenty five dinghies.

Races are held for these three classes with a Yeoman class as well planned for 1994. Racing starts in March and continues into October: throughout much of the season there is racing every Saturday and Sunday and on Wednesday evenings too. Highlights include the open regatta to start the season off in April and 'Final Fling' open regatta at the end of September, with in between a Schools Regatta and, for members only, races for the Loch Earn Cup held over two days in June, and a race to Lochearnhead and back.

Hertfordshire Scouts have been sailing on Loch Earn regularly for thirty years or so: their Wayfarers are a familiar sight.

The loss of the Loch Earn & Coastal Sailing School, formerly based at St Fillans, is much to be regretted. Established in 1960 by Lt.-Col. A. Campbell-Crawford, it became the first RYA-approved sailing school in Scotland, with some thirty residential pupils a week during its heyday in the sixties and seventies. It gained a notable reputation for good teaching. Even a prospective pupil's parents, attending for a couple of days to see what he would be learning, got the full treatment, capsize drill from the Mirror dinghy and all... *I* know. And quite right too!

By the late 1980s, more and more power boats were using the eastern part of the loch, and it became increasingly difficult to teach sailing while being buzzed by them, even though their drivers were probably unaware of the problems they were causing. With that and with residential sailing courses faced with competition from package holidays elsewhere, the sailing school has not outlived its sailing master's retirement a few years ago.

Water Skiing

Water Skiing has been a feature of Loch Earn for almost forty years. It dates from 1955 when Ewen Cameron, already running the Lochearnhead Hotel, gave his wife Ann a motor boat for a wedding present. This was powerful enough to tow someone on skis, or indeed on anything else suitable, such as an old car bonnet, upside down. The following year a water skiing club was formed, the first in Scotland and one of the first in Britain. It rapidly became a success story, with championships held at Lochearnhead and Cameron as chairman of the British Water Ski Federation from 1965 to 1970.

The present Watersports Centre replaced the old ski club in 1980, offering a range of activities among which water skiing at all levels has always been prominent. (For activities now on offer, see 'Waterside Facilities'.) Complete beginners learn by holding onto a training boom projecting from the side of the ski boat: alongside the instructor and close enough to hear his spoken instructions. The boat has an inboard engine and a safety platform at the stern for ease of getting in and out.

At the opposite extreme of skills, championships continue to be held: the BWSF Inland Ski Race Championships were held here in 1993, and are planned for 1994: from the 1993 results, the British team for the World Championships was selected.

Vintage water skiing. (STB/The Still Moving Picture Co.)

What Lies Ahead?

TOM Weir in *The Scottish Lochs*, published in 1971, commented on conflict of interests upon Loch Earn, and suggested that zoning was necessary. Ronald Faux, in an article with the somewhat alarmist headline 'Loch Earn is playground for a million', reported local concerns about the same problem in *The Times* for 11 March 1980. Yet here we are in 1994 and little has been achieved.

A Loch Earn Users' Association was established in 1967, but by 1981 was dormant. Comparable associations produce voluntary codes of conduct to regulate boats on Loch Tay and Loch Lomond. Windermere has been provided with full-scale byelaws.

Loch Earn in recent years has become to some extent a victim of its own success in attracting boats. Although its actual accident record could be a lot worse, the potential for serious accidents where power boats operate on crowded waters is all too evident, and has been brought sharply into focus by the tragic fatal after-dark collision between two power boats on Loch Lomond in 1993. There is now a reluctance noticeable among some owners of slipways to allow power boats and jet skis to be launched. Closure of the sailing school has been noted. When the last hirer of anglers' boats at St Fillans died his business closed too. But if the loch is becoming self-regulating for want of anything better, it is only doing so by discouragement of visitors who might, if things were better arranged, come to enjoy it.

The loch is also to some extent self-zoning, with more positive results: the maximum wind in which people can water ski in comfort is I understand about force 3, which is just about the point at which many sailors are getting interested. It is no coincidence that the loch's principal location for water skiing is at its western end, in the wind shadow offered by the land from the prevailing wind, while the sailing club is much further down the loch. Those power boat drivers who do use this part of the loch are often gentlemanly enough to keep to the south shore, and to keep out of the way of sailing races.

Nevertheless, problems have not gone un-noticed by officialdom. Ever since the *Marchioness* disaster on the Thames in 1989, the Department of Transport Marine Office (which becomes the Marine Safety

The head of the loch, looking to Lochearnhead.

Relax by the water, Lochearnhead.
(Loch Lomond, Stirling & Trossachs Tourist Board)

Agency in April 1994) has been reviewing in detail the safety of vessels and their users in and around Britain. Its West of Scotland Marine Safety Committee has an Inland Lochs Sub-Committee which is aware of problems on Loch Earn.

The Loch Lomond & Trossachs Working Party found on Loch Lomond problems similar to those of Loch Earn, and on a far greater scale. It recommended bye-laws - for boat licensing, speed limits, zoning, insurance, wardens and so on. It also noted that these might export Loch Lomond's problems elsewhere, for instance to Loch Earn.

Scottish Natural Heritage, too, is concerned with access to inland lochs for boating, as part of its wider concern with access to the countryside.

Opinions about what should be done, on Loch Earn as elsewhere, range from a national motor boat & driver licensing scheme, to minimal formal regulation - education rather than legislation. St Fillans Community Council is producing a set of common sense guidelines for use of Loch Earn; principal recommendations are covered above.

In the long run, bye-laws seem the most likely option. Powers are available, under the Civic Government (Scotland) Act 1982, section 121, to district councils to make bye-laws relating to inland waters. Perth & Kinross District Council drafted bye-laws for Loch Tay in 1989, but was unable to proceed. Stirling and Dumbarton District Councils are seeking bye-laws for Loch Lomond to cover collision regulations, control of access for launching, boat registration, speed, noise, etc. Should they be successful in obtaining them, it is likely that similar bye-laws would soon follow for Loch Earn, obtained by Stirling and Perth & Kinross District Councils which are in touch with one another.

Unfortunately it is unlikely that this attempt to promote bye-laws for Loch Lomond will be successful, for the same reason that Perth & Kinross District Council's attempt was unsuccessful: the Civic Government (Scotland) Act is defective. It requires the assent to proposed bye-laws of all riparian landowners who can be traced. It appears, therefore, that any intransigent owner of say 50 ft of foreshore who objects to introduction of bye-laws - or perhaps objects that they do not go far enough - has a power of veto.

It may well be that the attempt will fail for this reason, and that in turn may serve as a lever for the law to be changed. There is, however, in the author's

Skiing up the loch.
(Loch Lomond, Stirling & Trossachs Tourist Board)

opinion, another defect in the Act: it enables byelaws to be made only for pleasure craft. The latter apparently are not defined, and even if they were it is difficult to see how collision regulations, for instance, could be applied to pleasure craft but not to commercial vessels. The point would have limited application on Loch Earn, but would certainly be important on Loch Lomond. If the law is to be changed, those promoting the change should consider it.

The disadvantage to introducing bye-laws is the risk that the cure might be worse than the disease. They would be a restriction on individual liberty. They would be bureaucratic, and expensive to enforce. Registration of boats, with licence fees, would be needed, and wardens with boats for enforcement. But Windermere registration fees are said to cover administration costs, and produce a surplus to be ploughed back. On Loch Earn, wardens in boats might also form the basis of a full-time rescue service, and liaise with fishing wardens, and with the Police about security of boats and lochside properties. In the long term, one can dream of funds becoming available for construction of sheltered public harbours at Lochearnhead and St Fillans.

At any rate, that appears to be the position at the time of writing, early in March 1994. By the time you read this, there is likely to have been progress, in one direction or another. Perhaps.

In the meantime, please

Go Carefully,
Think of others' pleasure too,
Enjoy Loch Earn.

Further Reading

Beauchamp, E., *The Braes o' Balquhidder* Heatherbank Press, Milngavie, 1981;

Duckworth, C.L.D., & Langmuir, G.A., *Clyde River and Other Steamers* Brown, Son & Ferguson Ltd, Glasgow, 1972;

Lindsay, J., *The Canals of Scotland* David & Charles, Newton Abbot, 1968;

Loch Lomond & Trossachs Working Party *The Management of Loch Lomond and The Trossachs* Scottish Office, Edinburgh, 1993;

McNaughton, D.B., *Upper Strathearn From Earliest Times to Today* Jamieson & Munro;

McKerracher, A., *Perthshire in History and Legend* John Donald, Edinburgh, 1988;

Morrison, I., *Landscape with Lake Dwellings: The Crannogs of Scotland* Edinburgh University Press, 1985;

Murray, Sir J., & Pullar, L., *Bathymetrical Survey of the Scottish Fresh-water lochs* Challenger Office, Edinburgh, 1910;

Porteous, A., *Annals of St Fillans* David Phillips, Crieff, 1912;

Power from the Glens Scottish Hydro-Electric plc, Edinburgh;

St Fillans: a guide with maps St Fillans Community Council, 1991;

Shearer, J., *Antiquities of Strathearn* 1836;

Webster, D., *Scottish Highland Games* Reprographia, Edinburgh, 1973;

Weir, T., *The Scottish Lochs* Constable, London, 1970;

Wilson, J.S.G., *A Bathymetrical Survey of the Chief Perthshire Lochs and their Relation to the Glaciation of that District* Scottish Geographical Magazine, 1888;

Windermere (Lake) Byelaws South Lakeland District Council, Kendal.

Acknowledgements

Many people have been most helpful in providing information for this booklet, and I am particularly grateful to the following:

Maurice Baker, Ewen Cameron, Lt-Col. A. Campbell-Crawford, James Fraser, Arthur Henry, Winifred Henry, Patrick Laughlin, Dr James Martin, Lachie MacGregor, Elizabeth MacKinnon-Taylor, Capt. A. Munro, Robin Paterson, Andrew Salmond, Bobby Salmond, Duncan Scott, John Stewart, Sandy Stewart, Bobby Watson;

Proprietors and staff of lochside commercial establishments;

Staffs of: Local History Library, Perth; Scottish Library, Edinburgh; Drummond Estates; Royal Yachting Association; Scottish Hydro-Electric plc.; Scottish Natural Heritage; Central Regional Council; Department of Transport, Marine Office; Loch Lomond, Stirling & Trossachs Tourist Board; Perth & Kinross District Council; Perthshire Tourist Board; Stirling District Council; Tay River Purification Board; Tayside Regional Council;

and my family for their help and encouragement.

John Marshall has kindly prepared the artwork for the map. Pictures not otherwise acknowledged are by the author.